MW00633618

To Life!

A Collection of Prayers from Ramtha

Horus Publishing, Inc.

Compiled by
Diane Munoz-Smith

To Life!

© 1992 and 1996 Diane Munoz-Smith

All rights reserved. Printed in the United States of America. No part of this book may be reproduced or transmitted in any form or by any means without prior written consent of the publisher, excepting brief quotes used in connection with reviews written specifically for inclusion in magazines or newspapers. This work is derived in part from Ramtha Dialogues®, a series of magnetic recordings authorized by JZ Knight, with her permission. Ramtha® is a trademark registered with the U.S. Patent and Trademark Office.

ISBN 0-9652621-4-6

Published by
HORUS PUBLISHING, INC.
Suite 39, P.O. Box 7530
Yelm, WA 98597, USA
(360) 458-1440
Email: golden@yelmtel.com

Other Books by Diane Munoz-Smith and Horus Publishing, Inc.:

The Ancient Schools of Wisdom - A Selection of Teachings from Ramtha
(*The Ancient Schools of Wisdom* is also available in the German and Spanish languages.)

Photographs on pages 6, 148 and 149 by Marc Hazewinkel.
© JZK, Inc. All photographs courtesy of JZ Knight/JZK, Inc.

Acknowledgements

To Ramtha, the most outrageous, unusual, thorough and loving teacher I have ever known. Thank you for teaching me so well. There are no words to express the depth of the love and appreciation I have for you.

To JZ Knight, thank you for allowing this entity to come through you in this time and everything you've done to provide an excellent environment for him to do so.

To Greg Simmons of RSE Products & Services. Thank you for all your support, humor and great advice.

To Daved and Brien Munoz, my sons, whom I love greatly.

To my husband, Peter and my friends, Kim Smith, Caroline Couture.

And last but never least, Cheri Wentworth. Thank you for your constant encouragement and respect for my talents. It has always inspired me to reach beyond what I thought I could do.

Dedication

To the mornings and evenings of your days, that they be filled in between with the reality expressed in these pages.

—Diane Munoz-Smith

Contents

O my beloved God,
I am Ramtha, the Enlightened One,
for it is I who speak as that which is termed
the Lord of the Wind.
And unto that which is called
the four corners of the earth,
I draw nigh unto me this hour.
And that all these words,
these vibratory sounds
that come into being,
yea, indeed, they may manifest
that which they represent straightaway,
for my word shall be honored
and my truth shall be known.
And that which I teach,
indeed, my people shall experience
forthrightly,
for so say I,
Ramtha the Enlightened One.
So be it.

A Short History

JZ Knight had an extraordinary event happen to her one Sunday afternoon in 1977. In the middle of her kitchen appeared a glittering seven-foot being that only she could hear and see. He told her, quite simply, "Beloved woman, I have come to help you across the ditch." After the initial shock had subsided, the being, whose name was Ramtha, proceeded to explain to her who he was and what he was here to do.

35,000 years ago, Ramtha was a young boy living in Onai, a port city of Atlantis. As a Lemurian, he was forced to live in squalor and abject poverty, being treated worse than a common dog on the street.

At the age of twelve he had the devastating experience of burying the last of his family, his mother and infant sister, who had starved to death as a result of the Atlatian laws. Embittered and filled with hate and anger, Ramtha set out to do battle with the God of his people, the Unknown God, whom he felt had deserted his family and his race. The only place he knew to do battle with this God was to go to the highest mountain he could find, so he set out on the long journey with nothing but his hate to keep him going.

It took him two years to trek his way to the mountain and back. Once he arrived he cursed and threatened the Unknown God; there was no response. As Ramtha broke down and cried out to know why his people had been deserted by a God they revered, a beautiful woman appeared. She gave Ramtha a sword and told him to conquer himself.

Ramtha marched down from the mountain with a vengeance, the huge sword given to him in tow and a terrible light in his eyes. When he arrived in Onai he stormed the gates and razed the city to the ground. The other Lemurians in Onai gathered around him and demanded that he become their leader. Together they formed the fiercest army that ever walked this plane and waged war against all tyrants. By the end of his lifetime, Ramtha's army had grown to two million strong and they had conquered two-thirds of the known world.

Ten years into his march, Ramtha and his army had won every battle they had engaged. Wherever he went, his terrible reputation preceded him; most believed the rumor that he was immortal. During this time the army had come upon a peaceful valley and decided to set up their encampment.

After they had been settled for three months or so, an emissary approached the encampment and requested Ramtha to meet with the council of the palace in the nearby city of Nabor. It was their hope that they could come to an agreement for a peace treaty. The Ram agreed to come to their city to negotiate.

Once in the palace and summoned to the council room, Ramtha was asked to leave his sword behind for this was a meeting of peace. Bowing to their request, he handed over his sword. Before he knew what was happening (but after he had the pleasure of insulting the council's arrogance), a man from behind ran him all the way through with a sword, which was then pulled out, leaving him to die.

Through sheer determination and will, Ramtha survived the attack. He was able to jam his fist into his gaping wound, stopping the flow of blood, and forced himself to stand up. His attackers were horrified! They were now sure that the rumors that he was immortal were true. They fled in fear. He sent a servant for his men, who gathered him up and took him back to his camp and placed him in the care of the legion of women.

For seven years Ramtha sat on a rock convalescing, suffering the degradation of being taken care of by women. His wound was so great and painful he could neither sleep nor move his body without assistance. With little strength left and being forced into solitude, he had nothing else to do but contemplate nature. Through this contemplation and examination of the life that teemed around him, the Ram came to understand who and what the Unknown God was.

When he finally came off the rock, he had reached such a state of enlightenment that he dedicated the rest of his lifetime to live what he had learned. In the sixty-third year of his march, Ramtha gathered his people around him, and for one hundred and twenty days he communed with them and taught them what he had learned. On his last morning the great Ram danced his ideal of the morning sun and, as it rose, he ascended, promising to return.

*R*amtha's plan for his return to his people was to continue teaching them what he taught them so long ago. His plan meant that JZ (his daughter during his lifetime) would allow him to use her body to teach. The most important reason for this was to present a being that could not be seen and therefore not worshiped, for there was no form for the people to see. It would also demonstrate that God was neither male nor female and that God was the obvious unobvious, that which we could not limit to an identity.

And so in 1978, with JZ's agreement, Ramtha began holding Dialogues, teaching those who heard the call, his people of old. In 1988 he founded his School of Enlightenment, located on JZ's ranch in Yelm, WA, which continues this day.

Forward

There is nothing more powerful than to open your day with a prayer, setting forward into the day that which you wish to experience. Ramtha is well-known for his prayers. Not only is his love of God mighty, but so is his understanding of the circumstances that we are in. When Ramtha begins each session of his audiences, he uses the prayer to inspire and focus us into the day's lesson, for he knows that it is the Spirit within us that brings forward what we ask into our lives. When we accept his invitation to salute God with him, we are allowing ourselves to access the same essence he is, bringing forth a powerful declaration of our intent.

Contained within these pages are the prayers gleaned from ten years of audio tapes. I invite you to use them on a daily basis as a means to realign yourself with your desire to know and understand the God within you. Enjoy!

The Opening Prayer

This that we do, that which you have called prayer to God, it is how we salute the God within, and we do it with water, for water is that which is termed the knowledge of life. It represents that which is termed the flowing of consciousness from within to without. We begin each day to celebrate that which is termed the Lord God within your being.

This drink, as it were, is a salutation to the God within you for it is that unknown mysterious entity, as it were, that is the reason for this school. So we are saluting your potential; we are saluting God that lives within you. When you repeat the words, find passion in your being.

The power that a human being has to elicit their God is extraordinary, but it comes when the whole human is focused on being the word before it is ever uttered. Then it becomes a commandment.

Be the word that is given this day. Feel it before it issues forth from your mouth, that that which is spoken may be so.

True prayer has nothing to do with, indeed that which is termed words. Words are the shadow of truth in expression. True prayer is feeling the creation of the word. And this day, we have true prayer to begin this school.

Words, they be cripplers to truth. They are communication, but verily they do not express one's inward desire. One's inward desire often goes unexpressed because the words are inadequate for the expression.

Words, they are not of any accord. They are but sounds that have been remembered and taught as language to represent something visible, an action or a feeling. But words, as a language, do not constitute realism, for you say them without contemplating the depth of their meaning. So language on this plane has been the ultimate communicator. What you are going to learn is that they cripple the grandest expression.

Now in offering up that which is termed an invocation to something grand within you, you cannot simply say the word, you must feel its import. You must feel its meaning. When that is embraced, then this dedication will manifest; otherwise, it is best not to evoke this invocation. Feel the word before you say it.

Indeed, we bring forth that which is termed the word. Feel the word. Embrace the word. Let the word become manifest in your life. For the words of your toast, they be not idle chatter and they be not worthless; they manifest if they are embraced from within.

Speak the word with emotion, repeat the word with passion. Be the word in its totality, that that which is focused upon and defined by energy, that it may be so.

—Ramtha

What is God?

God be the all in all,
the Mother/Father principle;
that that principle is immutable,
that it is omnipresent,
that it is, in essence, mind.
The greatest and most unfathomable journey yet
is in the mind as absolute reality maker.
And he that discovers and experiences
this understanding will understand
what the kingdom of heaven is all about.

—Ramtha
April 1990

*N*ow don't start this prayer today with just repeating it because you're hearing me mouthing it and let me have all the passion. It's time for you to repeat the word slowly with your eyes closed and feel the word. Get a feeling for what you are saying, that what you are saying is that which you desire, utterly and completely. Then this prayer that we do is not an empty ritual, it is impaled with meaning, the heat of desire and the momentum of life. This is what you all want and for what you came here. You can have none of these unless you are a full participant in the prayer.

*A*nd every time we do this, this is the moment that we set aside our humanity and we speak to our God as a divine being. That is power. Contribute this to the power of yourself.

*C*lose those eyes.

—*Ramtha*

O my beloved God, mysterious One,
that which you are
has given me a life of expression
and significant purpose.
I often know that I am human,
who views you as distant and remote.
I ask you, my God,
to measure my work,
to enlighten my mind
and make my path straight,
for this I desire, to manifest you
in unequal and unchangeable terms.
This I ask,
that you bless me these days
and manifest my thoughts
straightaway.
So say I
from the lord God of my being.
So be it.
To life!

—*Ramtha*
November 1, 1996

To Life!

*Let us dedicate
the waters of life
to righteous truth,
for truth be
the river of life.
May the hour of truth
and freedom come.
So be it.*

—Ramtha

O my beloved God,
I do decree
that that which I focus upon ~~that is~~ CONSTRUCTIVE
I surely want.
Manifest it straightaway.
So be it.
To life!

—Ramtha

To the glory of God,
to the belovedness of Christ,
and to the resurrection of my mind,
unto the glory of my life
and my dominon over all things
to harness fate and to be destiny
and to ride with the wind,
to have at my fingertips
the change of universes and
to be lordship over them all,
to live unto forever,
to see the epics come and go,
to be that which is termed
a cloud of love
that it penetrates into the soul.
Ah, to be a Christ.
So be it.
To life!

—Ramtha

God bless my life.
God open my brain.
And God help me
to follow the path.
So be it.
To life.

—Ramtha

O my beloved God,
see into my soul,
unto my mind,
and cleave from that place
that which is
limitation.
Of this day
I do invite
you to my consciousness.
Make me worthy
of my destiny.
God bless my life.
So be it.
To life!

O my beloved God,
I call forth
that which I learn
this day.
I expect
to experience it.
God bless my life.
So be it.
To life.

—Ramtha

My beloved God, mysterious One,
I, that which is termed my humanity,
desire and struggle
to understand.
I beseech you this day
to fill me with your holy Spirit,
to enlighten me
to broader understanding
and set me free
of my doubt
and disbelief.
So say I
from the lord God
of my being.
So be it.
To life!

—Ramtha

From the lord God of my being
unto the glory within,
unto my reality
that I consume in life,
may it glorify and reflect
the power,
the beauty,
and the grace
that the lord God of my being
surely is.
To life!
So be it!

—Ramtha

O my beloved God, love I you greatly,
who hath loved me,
who hath been the fire in my sword,
who hath been the blue in my mantle,
who hath been the life
when death should have plucked my bones.
O my God, it has given me strength,
when I should have been weak and failed.
O my God, it is you
who hath made me worthy,
for I am nothing without you.
And you are the one that hath showed me
silver in a bird's wings across the moon.
And it is you who hath made
the clouds like phantoms over the hills.
And it is you who let me see the evening,
and hear the musicians of the water creatures
in their nightly serenade.
It is you who allowed me
to slumber in the bough of a great tree.
O my beloved God, love I you greatly.

—Ramtha

O my beloved God,
mysterious One,
this day
come I to learn,
to understand,
to experience.
My beloved God,
emerge within me
to open my limited mind
to fantastic
realism.
O my beloved God,
this day
flow from me
and open me up.
So be it!

—Ramtha

O my beloved God,
O my beloved Spirit,
of that which has created me,
such is your power
that hath hung the moon
in forever.
I desire of you
to change me
and remove my blocks,
present my limitations,
and give me the courage
to conquer them.
So say I
from the lord God of my being.
So be it.
To life.

—Ramtha

My beloved God, O my God!
hear me this day,
for unto me arise and shine.
Humbly open up my mind,
indeed, unlock my soul,
that I may understand.
And empower me, beloved one,
to experience mine understanding.
O my God, O my God,
I give thanks
for my life.
To you this day, dedicated am I.
So be it.

—Ramtha

My beloved God,
that lives within me,
of this day
I am uncertain,
thus call upon you
to fill my being
with peace,
knowledge,
and love.
And that which I learn this day
manifest it for me
straightaway.
God bless my life.
So be it.
To life!

(handwritten: you want for me)

—R₁

O my God
who gave me life,
unto that which I am
you are mysterious One.
For all the ways that I held you,
indeed, beheld you,
I have separated you from I.
I pray this week
to close this gap
and ask for your inspiration
and allow me to surrender.
Of all that I learn,
I ask of you
to manifest straightaway,
that this I may know
is the truth of your being.
So say I
from the lord God of my being.
So be it.
To life!

—Ramtha

O my beloved God,
that which is within me,
mysterious One,
of this day
I desire
to feel your presence.
Of this day
I dedicate my life
to your will.
Of this I do ask,
that all that I shall learn, EVER ~~learn,~~ *cannot*
by our will manifest it
that I may experience
and know truth.
God bless my life.
So be it.
T.

O my beloved God,
O mysterious One
I do feel.
Remove my ignorance
and my fear of joy
and let it be my comforter
and with that
knowledge,
experience,
wisdom.
My beloved God,
so be it.

Ramtha

O my God, my beloved,
unto this hour my soul sings!
My Spirit rejoices!
My mind hungry!
O my beloved God,
fill me with the fire
of completeness!
O my beloved God,
walk in me, of me; be me!
O my beloved God,
desire I to know and understand
that which man cannot know.
My beloved God, love I you greatly,
forever and ever and ever.
So be it.

—Ramtha

O my beloved God,
the endowment of that which I am,
I dedicate this week
to my enlightenment.
I dedicate my body
and my brain
to unfoldment.
And all that I study this week comes from "you"
I accept
in manifested form.
So say I,
from the lord God of my being.
So be it.
To life!

—Ramtha

O my beloved God,
let me humbly speak of my omnipotent Spirit.
I say you are holy, holy, holy.
Of your kingdom, your spiritual kingdom,
I desire to live within.
I call it forth, this kingdom of the divine,
that it may be manifest on earth.
O holy Spirit, of that which you are
I give to you this week my humble life.
I allow, indeed, invite you to come forward
and to make known your eternal destiny.
O my God, the goals of my life
are meaningless.
Therefore I give to you my permission, my will,
to make your goal known.
Empower me with all that I learn.
I accept every word into instant manifestation.
I eagerly await my spiritual path,
to experience these runners,
these manifestations.
Of every word and every feeling,
of my life to come, your kingdom come,
I now accept from the humanity of my being.
So say I. So be it. To life.
—Ramtha

O my beloved God,
beloved of my being,
O my Christ, ideal of my being,
listen unto me this hour.
Lift me up, that I may hear.
Lift me up, that I may know.
Give me the wisdom to understand
and be my God against fear.
O my God
that is within me,
awaken this day,
that this day
may be the beginning
of forever and ever and ever.
O my God, love I you greatly.
So be it.

O my beloved God, mysterious One,
call I from a distant place.
That which you be I am experiencing.
My beloved God, in great sincerity,
I do not desire to die yet.
My hour is coming to bloom.
I command you, I plead with you,
open up your bosom!
And let the waters of my life flow to me.
O my beloved God, how many hours did I not see?
How many nights did I not dream?
How many seasons did I lock away?
How many moments did I not understand?
Ah, 'tis a regretful feeling.
I am blooming. I am understanding.
Enjoin my life in your bosom,
that I might see, hear, know, understand, and live
to the epic of my being!
O my beloved God,
let it be, forever and ever and ever.
So be it.

—Ramtha

O my beloved God,
that which I am
hath been uncertain,
for I know not that which I am,
from whence I come,
the purpose of my beingness
and to that which I go.
My beloved God,
I am my greatest mystery!
This day desire I
to unravel this mystery.
Let all that is given to me
manifest for the glory of you,
my beloved God,
and, indeed,
my awakening.
So be it.

—Ramtha

O my beloved God,
now that I have found you,
I hear whispers in the marketplace
of your residence.
And I have looked high and low, near and far,
and, lo, I have found you within me all along.
What great jubilance; my soul cries out in joy!
O my beloved God within me,
let me embrace you; let me cry in your bosom;
let me laugh in your foreverness.
O my beloved God, you have become my passion.
I so desire that I am absorbed in you.
I am so desired to be that which you are glorified.
O beloved One,
rise me up higher than my greatest limitations,
my greatest weakness.
Make me a man amongst men,
a woman amongst women.
O my beloved God, sanctify me.
Show me righteousness. Let me live it.
O my beloved God, long I, desire I
to know that which you ar

This is my passion, that that which you
'tis my desire to be it ri

O my beloved God,
mysterious One,
that which is within me,
unto this day
I begin this work.
All that I learn,
indeed, all that I experience,
let it manifest in my life,
for the glory of that which you are,
forever and ever and ever!
So be it.

Ramtha

O my beloved God, mysterious One,
that which has no face and no ~~names,~~
that which you are,
I ask of you this day
from the deepest part of my being,
that you enrich my life,
indeed, that you open my mind,
that that which you are may manifest
through me.
O my beloved God,
this I desire above all else,
to live within your most beauteous bosom.
My beloved God, I ask this fine morn
that that which I learn I may experience.
And make me humble, that I may understand.
Love I you greatly.
So be it.

So what say I to you, Spirit?
That I humbly give you my life
and I am anxious for my adventure.
O my beloved Spirit,
remember this moment,
that one fine day
we review it together and find
that this offering of my humble life
was indeed my greatest destiny.
So say I,
from the lord God of my being.
So be it.
To life!

—Ramtha

O my beloved God, O holy Spirit,
that which has created me
and given me life,
indeed given me will, that with this will
I have formulated my life,
indeed I have created my personality-self.
O my beloved God,
this day I desire to remember you
that hath created me
and given me this life.
I open my mind, my soul,
and humble my body.
And all that I shall learn manifest
that this I may know
is the truth of my Spirit.
So be it.
To life!

—Ramtha

From the lord God of my being,
unto the glory within,
unto that which be I,
glorify me this day.
Bring down the walls
and allow the power
and truth
to be lived.
Unto this day
and to the glory of God,
I am.
So be it.
To life!

—Ramtha

From the lord God of my being,
to all that I am,
unto the discovery of this journey
to know that which be I.
For the God that is within me, *THE SPIRIT*
I call forth
that the imageless being
take over my life
and make my path straight.
Unto this day, come forth
and open my mind and my book,
that I may know,
may be empowered to endure.
So be it.
To the God within me.

—Ramtha

From the lord God of my being,
I am.
And unto my world I create,
it shall be of harmony
and of love,
of grace,
and of light.
Be of my world,
for there is the comforter,
the lord God of my being.
So be it!

—Ramtha

From the lord God of my being,
unto that which is,
prepare me, my Spirit.
Open my mind,
indeed, my eyes,
indeed, my ears,
that I may hear,
see, know, experience,
all that is.
So be it!

—Ramtha

From the lord God of my being
unto the Christ within,
unto this hour,
that which I am
be not flesh-weakened,
be not Spirit-faint,
be not mortal-humbled,
my God, my God,
for that which I am this hour
is the lord God of my being!
So be it!

—Ramtha

From the lord God of my being,
to the lord of hosts,
to this hour, ennoble me,
to this hour, empower me,
to this hour, transform me,
that that which I be
be worthy
of the lord God
of my being.
So be it.

O my God, hear me!
I ask this hour
that you waken my mind
and let it shine.
O my God,
I ask to release the power,
to experience.
O my God,
lift me from my ignorance,
that I may know.
Shine my path,
that I may walk and experience
the completion of my destiny!
O my God, so be it.

—Ramtha

O my God,
beloved within me,
unto this hour
awaken me.
Let my eyes be your eyes;
let my ears hear what you hear;
let my mind know your mind;
let my soul be filled.
O my God,
love I you greatly.
Be my life
forever and ever and ever!
O my God!

—Ramtha

O my God, my beloved,
creator of my being, of my life,
I humbly come to you
to open me up,
to empower my limbs
to experience.
O my God,
be unto me a staff of strength
and a rod of power.
O my God,
I give thanks to you
as the lord God of my being
for my life.
To my God.
So be it.

—Ramtha

O my God,
creator of Gods,
creator of hosts,
creator of I,
love I you greatly,
for unto my being
I celebrate
my awakening,
my life,
forever and ever and ever.
O my God,
I thank you
for I.
So be it.

—Ramtha

O my God,
simple be my soul,
simple be my Spirit.
Arraign this simplicity
in the richness and the beauty
of life forever.
O my God,
I come not as a king,
I come not as a queen,
I come not fabled, but unknown,
simple.
This hour accept unto your bosom
this shining light,
for therein shall I dwell
forever and ever and ever.
O my God, love I you greatly.
So be it.

—Ramtha

O my beloved God,
I give thanks from
the lord God of my being
for that which be I.
I give thanks from
the lord God of my being
for my conscious life.
O my beloved God,
I give thanks for my power,
my knowingness,
my beingness,
for indeed I am nothing
without your bosom.
My beloved father,
love I you greatly.
So be it.

—Ramtha

O my God,
that which I be
I have not understood,
nor have I lived.
I have done, I have spoken,
and I have thought
in ignorance.
Upon my altar
I lay these aside.
O my God,
let my mind know truth.
Let my words be silent.
And let my actions
be my truth.
O my God, make it so.
So be it.

—Ramtha

O my God
within me this day,
come forth
that I may learn
and that I may know.
Unto that which be I,
I desire knowledge,
freedom,
and life
lived in joy.
Let it be so.
So be it.

—Ramtha

O my God,
I celebrate my life,
indeed, its changing color,
its rising emotion,
indeed, its profound wisdom.
O my God,
indeed, celebrate I
the life that is within me
and around me.
O my God,
let me appreciate it.
Let me laugh
and have a light heart
in these days.
So be it.

—Ramtha

O my God,
I give great thanks,
indeed appreciation,
for what I am discovering
about me.
This I have found
a new wonderment,
indeed a new honey,
that of myself I am pleased.
O my God,
that which I am
desires no blocks
and no limitations
to my possibilities.
Let my destiny be fulfilled.
Let my mind be ripened.
O my God,
from the lord God of

O my beloved God,
that from which I came,
I be lost and seeking,
for that which be I
is not fulfilled.
Desire I
to begin to awaken.
Give me the courage
to awaken,
to understand
and to live
that which you be.
From the lord God of my being,
make it so.
So be it.

Ramtha

O my beloved God,
that which has eluded me,
I have forgotten and do stray.
My beloved God,
I have been a weak person.
I have not walked in splendor.
I have not walked in truth.
And my thoughts,
they have not been the crown
upon my forehead.
My beloved God, this be I.
But know this this hour:
to identify, to express
and to revel in my divinity,
to the power within you,
be my greatest desire!
Never let me forget!
So be it!

—Ramtha

O my beloved God,
that which is within me, that which be I.
O my God, what have I been?
The envelope of flesh and its world
have left me longing and unfulfilled.
O my beloved God,
be I the spark of you?
Have I access to that which be you?
O my beloved God, be this a truth;
remove the veil
and flow through me like a river,
for I am empty!
Let that which I be
begin to unfold this day.
O my God,
ignorance be the great evil.
Fill me with knowledge,
forever and ever and ever!
So be it!

—Ramtha

O my beloved God,
I rejoice
in that which I be,
for surely life teaches
the one who sees the lesson.
I celebrate my learning,
my evolution
and my awakening.
O my beloved God,
mysterious One,
continue to unfold.
From the lord God of my being,
so be it.

—Ramtha

August 14, 1996

O my beloved God,
bless this day
and prolong my life.
And of these things
that I have changed,
of these that I desire,
bring them quickly.
So be it.
To life!

—Ramtha

O my beloved God,
mysterious One,
that which I be am unfolding,
that which I be am changing,
that which I be am transmuting;
that which I be, wise, joyful,
that which I be,
love that which you be greatly.
My beloved God,
unto that which is within me,
that sacred place,
I give humble thanks
for my calling,
for I have earned it.
So be it!

—Ramtha

O my beloved God,
mysterious One,
I be the child in growth and bloom.
Ere I have learned
that that which I do is to be fed
the hunger of experience,
indeed, my growth.
O beloved One,
I revel in this understanding.
Stay close in me, out of me.
Be the center of my thoughts,
my great guardian.
Be my comforter, my mother, my father.
O my beloved God,
lift me up
and allow my growth to quicken!
So say I
from the lord God of my being!
So be it.

—Ramtha

O my God,
I see,
I feel,
I'm experiencing
a resurgence.
O my God,
continue to lift me
above mediocrity.
O my God,
purify me,
that my thoughts
be infinite unknown
forever and ever and ever.
So be it!

—Ramtha

O my beloved God, hail unto you,
this that I be,
that I have called self.
Allow it to transmute.
It is written,
"Ask unto that which you be
and it shall come forth."
O my God, search my being,
search my sincerity.
Take away that which is gray.
Fill me with passion.
Fill me with tolerance.
Fill me with strength.
Fill me with that which is termed allowance.
Burnish me impeccable,
that, O my God,
what see you in I
will be worthy
of transmutation.
I desire it
        the lord God of my being!

O my beloved God,
let I always know
that what I have found of you
will live everlasting in me.
O my beloved God,
whose existence not
I understood,
I am understanding.
I ask,
from the lord God of my being,
that that which you be
continue in me
forever and ever and ever.
O my God, let it be.
So be it.

—Ramtha

O my beloved God,
O mysterious One,
that which I have never known
but am awakening
unto my beloved parent,
this day I evoke the grandness,
that which you be,
to intercede
and open me up.
O my beloved God,
desire I to know
that which you be,
indeed
that which I be.
Bring it forth!
So be it.

—Ramtha

O my beloved,
I speak to you
from the lord God of my being.
All that I learn this day,
all that I experience this day,
may it manifest
for the glory of God within.
May it manifest
for the glory of Christ
in all people.
My beloved God,
this day
make it so.
So be it.

—Ramtha

O my beloved God,
mysterious One,
I have been a traveler of nowhere.
My beloved God,
I desire an adventure unknown,
uncalculated and unlimited
by that which be I.
My beloved God,
open me up
that my potential, my possibility,
may be realized.
Comfort my image
and lull it to sleep,
and let it dream the dreams
of wisdom.
So say I,
my beloved God,
from the lord God of my being.
So be it.

—Ramtha

O my beloved God,
bosom maker,
where I have traveled,
alas, I have come afar.
My beloved God,
I ask in your name
that you anoint me
with the fire of initiation.
O my beloved God,
find in me trustworthiness
and strength,
of that which I desire to know.
Come upon me as a denizen,
as a wind,
to fill my being.
O my beloved God,
know I think
this change cannot happen,
indeed the anointment,
unless I ask.
Make it so.
So be it!

—Ramtha

O my beloved God,
that which be I this hour
am crossed the fence
and am in the field
of prophesy;
am unfolding unknown.
O my beloved God,
give me strength
that I dare not go back.
For give unto me the will
and the heart of a lion
to move forward, to unfold
that which cannot be expected,
indeed, that which cannot be predicted,
indeed, that which be
the delightful miracle.
O my God,
let this be my destiny.
So be it!
To the fields!

—Ramtha

O my beloved you,
mysterious One,
that which is not squared
or angled or circled,
that which is not formed, yet is formed,
O mysterious One,
radiant being of that which is termed I,
you are what I hunger for:
the union, the marriage.
O my beloved God,
infuse my being
with strength of experience,
to gain my wisdom.
Offer unto me knowingness,
a selection of divine choice.
Give unto me clear-sightedness
and nobleness of being,
that that which I surely am
may change and transmute
unto that which you sure¹
O my beloved C

—Ra

O my beloved God,
mysterious One,
unto that which you be,
awaken me,
enliven me.
My beloved God,
I have been a stranger in this land.
My beloved God,
I know not what be I.
I am asking to be comforted.
I am asking to be in life.
I am asking to be awakened.
My beloved God,
this I ask
from the lord God of my being.
So be it!

O beauteous One,
my beloved God,
solitary being
dancing behind the veils,
hearken unto me,
lover of my being.
Come forth into my life
with greater measure,
greater power,
and greater vision.
O beauteous entity,
mysterious One,
have your way with me.
So say I,
from the lord God of my being!
So be it!

O my beloved God,
deep mysterious One,
know you this hour
I have spoken unto you.
Desire I
in my dualism
to become one
with that which you be.
O my beloved God,
I know the veils;
rent them in two
and build a fire
within my soul
for this great work.
Desire I.
So be it!

—Ramtha

O my beloved God,
gaze I unto you
into a blackened mirror.
Into the void search I
for the voice that had called me.
O my beloved,
that which you be
come nearer to my being.
To that which I be,
bring nearer to your being.
O my beloved God,
continue to open
that which I be,
that that which I am
may experience, evolve,
and become the voice
of the void.
So be it.

—Ramtha

O my beloved God,
gaze I upon that which is termed you,
see I nothing.
Turn my ear to listen
to that which is termed you,
hear I nothing.
Turn that which is termed my nose
to smell that which is termed
the fragrance which is termed you,
smell I nothing.
My beloved God,
I am that which is termed
a wayward traveler
searching for home.
O obedient One, send me a beacon,
show me what to see,
teach me what to hear
and what to smell.
O my beloved God, teach me to know you.
Desire I this
from the lord God of my being.
So be it!
To home!

—Ramtha

O my beloved God,
that which is the
mysterious wonder of my being,
that gives unto my passionate heart
that which is termed life
that flows through my veins,
O my beloved God,
that which you are, magician,
make unto me all that you are.
Give unto me that which is termed
the heart that beats forever.
Give unto me that which is termed
the passion and the desire
to know all things.
Give unto me that which is termed
the ability to create and uncreate.
O my beloved God,
do with me as you will
to bring this desire
to its greatest apex.
So be it.
P.S.: I want to live through it.

—Ramtha

O my beloved God,
quiet One,
issue forth from me
with all your manifested desire.
When I am ready to surrender,
quicken your fire
in my being
that my life
extended hereto
shall know no end.
O my beloved God,
this I desire
from the lord God of my being.
God bless my life.
So be it.
To life!

—Ramtha

O my Spirit,
divine and mysterious,
I have come to learn
that you be
my deeper value.
I have been a fool.
I have wrought my life
with limitation and degradation.
O that which is beautiful of me,
O that which is eternal of me,
I humbly ask
that you interfere
with my foolish image
and strike my life
markedly divine, compassionate,
powerful, and loving.
O Spirit, eternal fire,

O my beloved God,
that which has created me
and given unto me life,
awaken in me
my passion to know.
Give back my power
that I may manifest
a journey,
a path
to enlightenment.
So be it.
To life!

Ramtha

O my Spirit, fire in my soul
that allows my life,
that allows my thought,
that moves my body
and quickens my joy,
I worship you. I adore you.
I invite you to govern my life.
Of the mystery in my book,
I've known not,
but I beseech you
with all my might
that you bring forth
my unknown destiny,
for yearn I,
Spirit of my being,
to know all,
to live without end,
to be empowered.
Of this I desire,
my beloved Spirit.
So be it.

—Ramtha

O my beloved God,
of that which I desire,
fill me to all eternity
of the adventure of life.
I swear
I shall not pass away
but shall live forever
in the Spirit
of your bosom.
God help my life.
So be it.
To life.

—Ramtha

O my beloved God,
I am like the butterfly
but I have glue on my wings!
God help me!
I desire to fly!
Teach me
to make them move!
So be it!
To life!

—Ramtha

O my beloved God,
who created me
and gave unto me
singular life,
I desire you empower me
with your will.
I desire
that your kingdom
be made manifest
through me.
For truly
no greater destiny have I
than to be
my beloved God.
So say I,
from the lord God
of my being.
So be it.
       'ife.

O my beloved God,
creator of my being,
giver of my reality,
I give you my will
to change me.
I give you my will
to evolve my reality.
This I desire
from the lord God
of my being.
So be it.
To life!

O my beloved Spirit,
holy One,
your kingdom
and your power
is omnipotent.
O my beloved Spirit,
I surrender unto you
my humble soul,
that you remake and reconsider
my destiny.
O my beloved Spirit,
that from creation,
abide in my life ever.
This I desire from you.
So be it.
To life!

—Ramtha

O my beloved God,
that which conceived my Spirit,
gave me the power of embodiment,
you are greater
than I have supposed.
Break down these barriers
and let your will,
your kingdom,
your power,
your mission,
be fulfilled in me.
God manifest this prayer.
So be it.
To life!

—Ramtha

O my beloved God,
that which you are,
I desire to be.
Of the mind that you are,
I desire to possess.
Of the immortality that you be,
I desire such a life.
And the love have you for I,
I desire for others.
God bless my life.
So be it.
To life!

—Ramtha

O my beloved God,
fill me with your Spirit,
that my boundaries
become unlimited.
O my beloved God,
I accept my runners,
all that I have focused upon,
and beckon it to me
straightaway.
O my beloved God,
fire in my soul,
let that which I am
be continued in my life.
So be it.
To life.

—Ramtha

O my beloved God,
point zero,
I have found you.
That which you are
I desire to embrace,
for desire I
new potentials.
Come forward.
So be it.
God bless my life.
So be it.

—Ramtha

O mind that is cosmic,
that engenders
all civilizations
far and near,
unto this hour
I call forth the unity
of my mind
with the great mind.
From afar, hear my voice,
open up thy abode
that my mind may enter
everlasting understanding
forever and ever and ever!
So be it!

—Ramtha

O my beloved Spirit,
my mighty Spirit, omnipotent One,
you who are filled with
the power of heaven and earth,
fill me with your power.
O my Spirit, fill me
with your manifested kingdom
that I may be a vassal
to bring forth
that which is unseen in heaven,
to subdue that which is seen on earth.
Manifest for me my daily food
that I may live to know my guilt,
my doubt, my sorrow,
and then realize the truth.
O mighty Spirit,
do not allow me to be tempted.
Protect me from all
that would persuade me.
And manifest through me
God divine.
So say I; so be it.
To life!
—Ramtha

February 23, 1996

To Life.

O my beloved Spirit,
I know that you are
my omnipotent being.
I know that you are
all powerful.
My Spirit,
I hunger for you
to fill me with
your beingness.
I want you to fill me
with your purpose today.
I want you to use me
as a vassal today,
to manifest
the agenda that you covet.
Let me be a vassal
to bring forth
your power in heaven.
So be it.

Healing
Mind, Body
& Spirit

O my God,
tis not that I fear,
but that I forget
what I am,
what I be.
It is a rough lesson
being my illusion.
I ask
that the power
come forward in me
to remind me
I am greater
than my illusion
of existence.
So be it.

—Ramtha

O my God, my beloved,
unto this hour
be I jubilant,
be I troubled.
Help me to understand
and to become grander.
Shine forth from my being
that my path is lit.
Welcome me home,
my beloved Father,
from that which be I,
awakened this day.
So be it.

—Ramtha

O my God,
I shiver in these days
of terrible shadows
and unsettling truth.
O my God,
I have been so blind at my awakening.
I am sickened in weakness
to my enemies.
O my God,
if love is the wine, let me be filled,
that within my being
the love that is lost
can be found,
and with my God be lifted up!
O my God,
help me to know this.
Indeed, help me to feel this.
O my God, love I you greatly.
So be it.

—Ramtha

O my beloved God within me,
ever show me your presence.
Walk as my life.
Create as my life,
that that which be I
can be called
the lord God of my being.
O my God,
lift me out of troubled water
and stand me on solid ground,
that my destiny may be fulfilled.
O my God, you are
the love of my being.
Love I you greatly.
Unto these things I do
this hour in my time,
they are of you.
And give me a testament
of the love of my God,
forever and ever and ever!
So be it!
—Ramtha

O my God,
my beloved,
uplift me from my sorrow,
from my pain,
from my sickness.
O my God,
uplift me from my limitation.
Bring me forth
and set me upon even ground.
My beloved Father,
empower this your child
to live the life
forever and ever and ever.
So be it!

O my beloved God,
I awaken to your joy
and I embrace happiness.
O my beloved God,
I have been a victim
of all my creation.
Help me to see
the purposefulness
and the rewards
so this that I have felt
can be at peace
forever and ever and ever.
So be it.
To life!

—Ramtha

O my God, banish my ignorance.
O my God, banish my image.
O my God, open me up,
that all I learn today
LOVE   TO YOUR KNOWLEDGE AW YOUR
I give permission to experience.
O my God,
heal my body this day.
O my God,
relieve my pain this day.
O my God,
unshackle my mind this day.
And this day
I dedicate to that which has sent me.
So be it.

—R

O my Spirit,
holy, holy, holy are you.
You are omnipotent;
you are eternal.
Hear me, I beseech you, hear me.
I command you,
my all powerful Spirit,
in my name,
to release me from
my past,
to free my mind
and to free my body,
that I may have radiant health.
I command you in my name
to do this swiftly.

antha

O my beloved Spirit,
omnipotent One,
holy, holy, holy one,
I am burdened
in my soul
and of my mind,
and I am sickened
in my life.
I know not what to do.
I give you this burden
and commend it into your hands.
So be it.

—Ramtha

Almighty, righteous,
and all-powerful Spirit,
I give to you my body;
make it perfect.
I surrender it to you for healing.
O beloved Spirit,
omnipotent One,
fill me with your power
and your perfection.
Exalt my humble
and diseased body
to radiant health.
So be it.

—Ramtha

O my God,
unto my being
I have been lost, I have been blind,
and I have not heard the music.
O my God,
this enslavement upon me
I order to be removed.
O my God,
to know what be you
I shall understand I.
Enough of my sadness,
of my pain, of my sorrow
that have weakened me so.
Open my mind.
Let me know truth
and let it be experienced,
for I that have been lost
desire to be found.
O my God, love I you greatly!
So be it!

—Ram'

O my beloved God,
it be a great truth:
I have been a blind wanderer.
I have not heard the music
or the whispers.
My beloved God,
I have felt lost no more.
O beloved One, restore my ~~brain,~~ mind
restore my soul, and heal my body.
Bring forth my path,
clearly trod by those before me.
Let my past be rolled up
into the book of my soul.
Let the page be turned;
let the writing begin.
O my beloved God,
I want to come home.
Make it so!

O my God,
my days are lengthened
for I am consuming
my past regression.
My soul is in bloom.
Shine forever,
that that which I am
shall eternally grow
and become the light
of the world.
O my God,
my days are lengthened.
My Spirit is born
forever and ever and ever!
So be it!

—Ramtha

O my God,
I celebrate my life.
I celebrate my awakening.
Let me not be tattered.
Let me not be torn.
Let me not despair.
O my God,
I am anew.
Bring forth the ~~unknown;~~ THY WILL FOR ME
give me strength
to engage it.
So be it!

—Ramtha

O beloved holy creative Spirit,
I long for your revelation.
Take me into my slumber,
I ask.
Heal my mind,
release my Spirit
and take my body this night.
I give it to you.
And when I awake,
I long to smell your fragrance
within me.
So be it.

—Ramtha

N

While I sleep,
O mighty One,
I give you my body
and my mind.
Heal me
and change me
and work these wonders,
that I arise anew.
So be it.

tha

O my beloved God,
mysterious One,
of this I understand
that I know very little,
and of that I understand
I have very little.
O my God,
change this in me
and open my mind
and my brain
to unlimited possibility.
This I ask
from the lord God
of my being.
So be it

—Ramtha

Twilight

O my God,
to be this day.
Open and engage
that I may know,
that I may understand,
that I may be uplifted.
O my God,
resurrect my being
from the deepness of sleep,
to the morning awakening.
So say I.
So be it.

—Ramtha

O my beloved God,
O mysterious One,
this wondrous eve
I celebrate
the closeness
that be you.
O my beloved God,
my longing,
my treasure,
flow through me
in willful breath.
Be unto me
destiny.
O my beloved God,
make my vessel pure.
So be it.

—Ramtha

O my beloved God,
Mother/Father
of that which is termed I,
O mysterious One,
raise me up this eve.
Remove my hardened heart
and my limited thinking.
And, beg, let me know
and understand,
for whence I go.
I say to you,
O great one,
that with deep sincerity
the answers will provide
a willing Spirit.
So be it!

—Ramth

O my beloved God,
mysterious One,
my holy Spirit,
that which has given me form,
life, and indeed will,
I salute you this night
and join with you my life
for evolution.
I desire that whatsoever I learn
this fine evening,
manifest it into my life,
for unto this
my life changes.
Love I you greatly.
So be it.

O my beloved God,
my divine Spirit,
I come this night
open-souled
and without grievance.
This night I dedicate
to your awesome power.
Move in me
to effect unto reality
your imperishable truth.
So be it.
To life.

—Ramtha

O my beloved God,
my holy Spirit,
quiver me with your energy.
Subdue my raging heart
and fill my soul
with your power,
my mind with your thoughts.
O my beloved Spirit,
I ask of you
to manifest for me
all that I learn this night,
for desire I evolution.
So say I,
from the lord God of my being.
So be it.
To life!

—Ramtha

O my beloved God,
I speak to you
from the lord God of my being.
This love,
this light-heartedness,
this jubilance of Spirit,
let it last night till many morns.
For truly this is living!
O my beloved God,
so it be a truth,
the greatest gift is love.
Love I you greatly!
So be it.

—Ramtha

My beloved God,
be my tower,
be my rock,
be my strength,
ever close,
ever near.
I have spoken these words
and perhaps do not understand fully
their meaning.
I cherish that which you are
and humbly ask that,
according to my reception,
be these things unto me this night,
forever and ever and ever!
So be it!

—Ramtha

O my beloved God,
this day I have grown.
This eve I am unfolding.
Change, my beloved God,
hath been a bitter fruit.
O my beloved God,
alas, it was only my fear.
Unfold me, Troubadour, unfold me!
Give me the strength
to understand
and the wisdom to choose.
So say I
from the lord God of my being,
forever and ever and ever!
So be it!

—Ramtha

O mysterious One,
beloved of my being,
what day of this day have I lived?
What day of this day did I not live?
O mysterious One,
be you all things
that I lived not this day?
I think so.
That which ask I of you,
teach me.
I evoke you
to bring forth understanding,
experience, and knowledge,
that this day
I will never miss.
Love I you greatly!
So be it!

—Ramtha

O my beloved God,
how have I defined you this day?
To what part
did you deliver my day?
And to what degree,
I beseech you,
did I receive?
O my beloved God,
ever bring forth unto that
which is termed I
the hunger to know,
the understanding
and life to live it!
Teach me humility
and the grand virtue called love,
that my days are lived fully
and that life
begat from my being
is rich in the reward of being.
So be it!

—Ramtha

O my beloved God,
sun of my being,
I do give thanks this day
for this that I have learned,
for I celebrate
this knowledge
as my freedom,
for I align myself
with my body
only through my Spirit.
God resurrect my Spirit.
So be it.
To life!

—Ramtha

O my beloved God,
to that which you be,
without form, without image,
unto that which you are,
I call you forth.
Open my door,
and, indeed, manifest
unto my humble being.
I evoke you
to consecrate my change
and purify me in fire,
that that which I offer up this night
shall manifest
for the glory of God,
the source, the principle
I am within me.
Love I you greatly!
So be it!

—Ramtha

O my beloved God
I do give thanks
this wondrous night
for my life.
And of this night
I am greatful
for all that I have learned
and invite you
to bring about
more adventure, more learning
and more life.
O my beloved God,
teach me to forgive myself
of my unworthiness
to celebrate this prayer.
So be it.
To life!

—Ramtha

O my beloved God,
I give thanks for this day,
for I am so honored
to participate
in my own journey.
O my beloved God,
I do accept
my focus this day,
and bar from me
any resentment.
So say I,
from the lord God
of my being.
So be it.
To life.

—Ramtha

O God of my dream,
far in the netherworld,
come upon me,
possess me,
direct me,
and manifest me
to your law.
So say I,
from the lord God
of my being.
So be it.
To life.

—Ramtha

O my God,
salute I Ra,
who has glistened the horizon
with deepening hue.
My Spirit in slumber
soars at midnight,
for blessed has been this day
that I have lived.
May it come again
forever and ever and ever!!
So be it!

—Ramtha

Christ-In-Mass

O tree of Christ,
that lives in my soul
and now in my hovel,
what be you?
Be you the symbol of everlasting life
that I have adorned
with my images of beauty?
O tree of Christ,
allow my adornment
to color your world,
for I have not the eyes
to see the color
that you radiate
in my soul, in my hovel.
O beloved tree,
be not a cross
but a tree to live
forever and ever and ever.
And in all my dreams, be there.
So be it.

—Ramtha

O my beloved God,
bless this night
the Christ-tree.
Give life this night to me.
Of the tree
give knowledge this night.
Of the tree,
my beloved God,
bring forth within me
my roots,
that they bear unto me
the understanding
and the knowledge
of sacredness.
O my beloved God,
let me see the tree
for what it is.
So be it.

—Ramtha

In memory of the Christ, O my beloved God
that which is within me,
I rise up and rejoice and celebrate
your illustrious son.
To the glory of Christ,
O my God, 'tis the celebration of love
and remembrance.
O my God, who love I greatly,
give me the courage,
the strength and the power
to know what your son knoweth.
O my beloved God,
to be unified, to be glorified in you,
this be my desire.
Hail, Jesus Christ,
King of kings and Lord of hosts.
I rejoice your birth
forever and ever and ever.
O my God, I am lifted.
To Life! So be it.

—Ramtha

Blessings

O my beloved God,
my beauteous Spirit,
love I you greatly.
Of that which I have learned,
I dedicate to you
and empower you
to change the direction
of my life.
O my beloved God,
give me more.
So be it.
To life!

—Ramtha

I send to you, unto your house,
your land, to your dreams
and to your mornings,
I send to your reality blessings
from the lord God of my being,
all your days in this fine year.

To all of its days
you shall be uplifted.
Unto your house,
and to your land,
and to your family,
to your being,

to your morning, to your evening,
I impose upon you the blessings
from the lord God Ram,
that you shall be lifted
all the rest of these days;
lifted higher and higher and higher.

Indeed! I bless you! I strengthen you!
I send my consciousness to you!
And that which you shall touch shall change!
And that which you walk shall bring joy!
And unto your place shall bring bounty,
and it shall be protected.

*And unto your life
you shall know joy.
For unto you,
from the lord God
of my being,
so say the Ram!
I do this thing!*

*You are my people, my beloved people,
and you have rallied,
and in the storm you have stayed tall,
and in the greatest tests
you have prevailed.
From these days forward
you will transmute and bring joy,
and unto your life it will be blessed
and no longer condemned.*

*Give unto the earth the blessing
that I have given you.
Transmute it, that you have been transmuted.
Celebrate your life!
For life, this life, is the expression
of your awakening.*

I love you. So be it.

—Ramtha

To the lord God of your being,
may this hour it have heard,
that it waits to be touched.
To the lord God of your being,
love I greatly
for its immortalness,
its power, and its love,
when it had none to give to.
To the lord God of your being,
be I your champion
for that which I know
and uphold and glorify,
forever and ever and ever.
So be it.

—Ramtha

Ixt lahng actin tu ahgdooglma.
Ihn mah amaroosh
Ihn thah agcandu thayoolsehmah,
ah lah uhm amaroosh,
Ram.

From me to you,
I love that which you are.
From God to God
and soul to soul
and unto this journey,
I love all that you do.
So be it.

—Ramtha

Other Ramtha Titles

The following is a list of books on Ramha available through RSE Products and Services and other fine book stores. Also available is a whole library of recordings of Ramtha's teachings. All products are available through mail order at:

RSE Products and Services
PO Box 519 • Yelm, WA 98597
(360) 458-4771 or (360) 458-2956
email: greg@ramtha.com
Website: http://www.ramtha.com

✷ RAMTHA   *Edited by Dr. Stephen Lee Weinberg (217 pages)* The classic work on Ramha, that Ramtha himself has referred to as "The Great White Book." A brilliant book designed to inform the general public as to the nature of Ramtha's teachings along with a rich sampling of his wisdom on many topics. Highly recommended for those ready to understand this great teacher and his message. It is one of the most important books to read if you are preparing to enter the school.
#1401 - Hard Cover $ 19.95
#1401 - Leather Bound Edition $ 29.95

✷ THE ANCIENT SCHOOLS OF WISDOM   *Compiled by Diane Munoz. (197 pages).* Taken from a 3-day weekend in May of 1988 where Ramtha set the foundation for his School of Enlightenment, which still is operating this day. An extraordinary account of the nature of reality, how time works, the history of the ancient schools of wisdom, their purpose, and how to live from your Spirit rather than your humanity, laying the seeds for living and unfolding wisdom in your life.
Soft Cover $19.95

✷ RAMTHA: AN INTRODUCTION   *Edited by Steven Lee Weinberg, Ph.D. (228 pages).* An engaging collection of teachings that will appeal equally to those familiar or unfamiliar with Ramtha. More than an introduction; a true treasure of personal mastery.
#1404 - Soft Cover $ 9.95

✷ LOVE YOURSELF INTO LIFE   *Edited by Steven Lee Wein-berg, Ph.D.* All who enjoy Ramtha's profound and eloquent teachings will cherish this comprehensive collection of work on a wide variety of topics culled from Ramtha's exchanges with people. Almost 500 pages. Destined to be a collector's item.
#1405 - Large Soft Cover Format $ 39.00

✱ I AM RAMTHA *Edited by Richard Cohn, Cindy Cohn, and Greg Simmons. (127 pages).* This book is a beautifully photographed book that accompanies thirteen of Ramtha's most universal teachings. Wonderful teachings on the subject of feelings, being at one with nature, unconditional love, and the prize that is called life.
#1201 - Hard Cover $ 9.95

✱ I AM RAMTHA *Edited by Richard Cohn, Cindy Cohn, and Greg Simmons. (127 pages).* Signed, Limited Collector's Edition No two alike. Each cover individually made with a combination of hibiscus, Hawaiian native herbs and 24K gold flake. The paper is handmade and the photos hand-selected. The spine is parchment and the book is bound by a man trained in the rare book section of the Vatican Library. A timeless treasure.
#1201-A - Special Order Only $ 99.50

✱ A STATE OF MIND *JZ Knight. (445 pages).* The intimate account of JZ's life in her own words. Her story, which includes her humorous and poignant introduction to Ramtha, is a story of the triumph of the human spirit. Also available in an edited audio version, recorded in her own voice *(120 minutes)*
#1501 - Hard Cover $ 9.95
#1501.1 - Cassette $ 9.95

✱ THE SPINNER OF TALES *Compiled by Deborah Kerins. (228 pages).* Ramtha has captivated audiences throughout the years with the telling of his tales. Now they have been put together in book form to be preserved and delight readers of all ages. These stories are from the earliest years of the teachings to the most recent. A true treasure! (#1 Book of 1991)
#1300 - Soft Cover $ 10.00

✱ THE LAST WALTZ OF THE TYRANTS *Edited by Judi Pope Koteen. (153 pages).* This book is a synthesis of Ramtha's teachings on the challenges we face by those who control the world economy and from the coming radical changes in nature. It provides inspiration and practical guidelines to enable you to be prepared.
#1202 - Soft Cover $ 11.00

✱ UFO'S AND THE NATURE OF REALITY: UNDERSTANDING ALIEN CONSCIOUSNESS AND INTERDIMENSIONAL MIND *Edited by Judi Pope Koteen. (221 pages).* This book is a sometimes shocking, sometimes comforting picture of what we would call alien intervention in our history, in our present, and in our future. It allows us to see what is "out there." But this is more than another UFO book. It exposes the limitations of subjective mind and encourages the

reader to move into inter dimensional mind, the source from which all is available. This book will alter the way you've perceived everything you've been told.
#1611 - Soft Cover $ 11.00

✳ CHANGE: THE DAYS TO COME   *Ramtha (149 pages)*. Based on the 3 day intensive taught in Denver, May 1986. This book tells of man's destruction of Earth's resources and nature's recourse to heal herself.
Soft Cover $ 10.00

✳ SOULMATES: THE INTENSIVE   *Ramtha. (128 pages)*. Based on the 3 day intensive taught by Ramtha in Seattle, WA, January 1986. This book spells out the mystery of the science of soulmates and its importance in the knowing and loving of self.
#1403 - Soft Cover $ 10.00

✳ BECOMING   *Edited by Khit Harding.* The second Ramtha book, now a classic of which there is a limited supply. A non-linear teaching on the becoming process
#1101 - Soft Cover $ 14.95

✳ MANIFESTING: A MASTER'S MANUAL   *Edited by Khit Harding. (100 pages)*. Based on the November 1986 intensive, The Power To Manifest, this is compiled such that each page serves as a thought-provoking concept for contemplation and understanding.
#1102 - Soft Cover $ 9.95

If you are interested in knowing more about Ramtha's School of Enlightenment, for a free introductory packet call or write to:

Ramtha's School of Enlightenment
PO Box 1210
Yelm, WA 98597
(360) 458-5201 ext. 10
email: audrey@ramtha.com
Website: http://www.ramtha.com

BAPTIZM

1ST I CORINT. 12:13
BAPT BODY OF CHRIST. BY HOLY CHRIST

2ND WATER BAPT.   ACTS 8. 34 - 36
BAPT   ACT 10:47   36 - 38

3. HOLY SPIRIT   MATHIEU 3:11
BAPT.   GOST   MARK 1:8
                LUKE 3:16
213 758 - 3777   JOHN 1:33
                ACTS 1:5 (JESUS)
                " 2:1-2 SPOKS
                        7IER
                ACTS 2:3-4.

a. WHO SHOULD BE BAPTIZED ?
   ACTS 2:38   FOR = BECAUSE OF.

R. 2 { EVERYBODY HOW ACEPT. JESUS !
      { AS SEVION
        ACTS 8:36-37
        ACTS 19: 3-5 PAUL AT EPHISOSS
WHY ?   4.
1. TO BE SAVED. MARK 16: 14-16
2HS RENSON   JESUS SAEY SO
        ROMANS 6: 3-6
   — DEATH AND RESURECTION
        COLOSSION 2

   } WBO1 Rok 90,000
        LA. ex.º 1000 º,
   DR. FREDRICK K. C. PRICE.